Seven CONTINENTS of the World

ANTARCTICA

By Tracy Vonder Brink

A Crabtree Crown Book

Crabtree Publishing
crabtreebooks.com

School-to-Home Support for Caregivers and Teachers

This appealing book is designed to teach students about core subject areas. Students will build upon what they already know about the subject, and engage in topics that they want to learn more about. Here are a few guiding questions to help readers build their comprehensions skills. Possible answers appear here in red.

Before Reading:

What do I know about Antarctica?

- *I know Antarctica is a continent.*
- *I know it is very cold in Antarctica.*

What do I want to learn about this topic?

- *I want to know how Antarctica was explored.*
- *I want to learn about animals that live in Antarctica.*

During Reading:

I'm curious to know...

- *I'm curious to know how much ice is in Antarctica.*
- *I'm curious to know how seals stay warm in Antarctica.*

How is this like something I already know?

- *I know how much ice is near my home in winter.*
- *I know how I stay warm in winter.*

After Reading:

What was the author trying to teach me?

- *The author was trying to teach me what kind of landforms Antarctica has.*
- *The author was trying to teach me how cold Antarctica is.*

How did the photographs and captions help me understand more?

- *The photographs helped me picture Antarctica.*
- *The captions gave me extra information.*

TABLE OF CONTENTS

CHAPTER 1
Get to Know Antarctica 4

CHAPTER 2
Landforms and Climate 8

CHAPTER 3
Natural Resources 14

CHAPTER 4
Plants and Animals 16

CHAPTER 5
Exploring Antarctica 22

CHAPTER 6
Antarctica Today 26

GLOSSARY 30

INDEX 31

COMPREHENSION QUESTIONS 31

ABOUT THE AUTHOR 32

CHAPTER 1
GET TO KNOW ANTARCTICA

What continent has the world's coldest temperatures? Where do penguins waddle and icebergs tumble into the sea? Where do no people live permanently?

Antarctica!

Antarctica sits at the bottom of the world. It is south of the **equator**. The continent is almost shaped like a circle, except for a **peninsula** that points toward South America. The South Pole is found on Antarctica.

The world has seven continents. Antarctica is the fifth largest.

OCEANS AND ICE

The Southern Ocean surrounds Antarctica. Ice shelves make up almost half of the continent's coasts. Ice resting on top of rock meets the water along other parts of the coast.

An ice shelf is a floating sheet of glacier ice connected to a landmass. Most of the world's ice shelves are found in Antarctica.

Antarctica is divided into two parts, East Antarctica and West Antarctica. The Antarctic Peninsula is the continent's northernmost point. Ice covers almost all areas of the continent.

CHAPTER 2
LANDFORMS AND CLIMATE

Mountains, valleys, and plains lie completely hidden underneath the ice. Only the highest mountains peek above the frozen surface. Lake Vostok, one of the world's largest lakes, is in Antarctica. Lake Vostok is not only frozen, it also sits underneath an ice cap.

Lake Vostok is buried under 2 miles (3.2 km) of ice.

Antarctica is frozen, but the inside of Mount Erebus stays hot. A lava lake full of molten rock sits at the volcano's top.

MOUNTAINS

The Transantarctic Mountains divide East and West Antarctica. Mount Vinson is the highest mountain in Antarctica. It is in the west. Mount Erebus stands on Ross Island. Mount Erebus is Earth's southernmost active volcano.

THE ANTARCTIC ICE SHEET

Antarctica is a rocky continent. The massive Antarctic Ice Sheet lies on top of the rock. This ice sheet holds 90% of Earth's ice. The ice is 3 miles (4.8 km) deep in some places. Seventy percent of the world's freshwater sits frozen there.

The Antarctic Ice Sheet is twice as big as Australia. If it all melted at the same time, it would raise sea levels by about 200 feet (61 m).

The iceberg that sank the Titanic broke off the Jakobshavn glacier in Greenland.

SEA ICE AND ICE SHELVES

Sea ice floats in the waters around Antarctica. Some sea ice is thin and melts away during summer. Others stay frozen all year and grow thicker in winter. Ice shelves are always attached to the land. Sometimes huge chunks break off, fall into the sea, and become icebergs.

CLIMATE

Antarctica has a dry polar **climate**. It is considered a desert. Antarctica is the coldest place on Earth. In winter, it is dark 24 hours a day. In summer, it's the opposite. However, the sunlight bounces off the shiny ice, so little warmth reaches the ground.

Parts of Antarctica are around -18°F (-28°C) even in the summer. Winters may be as cold as -144°F (-98°C).

Emperor penguins are the largest penguin. They stand nearly 4 feet (1.2 m) tall.

Antarctica is also the windiest place on Earth. Strong winds circle the continent. The winds blow from the frozen **interior** down the coasts. So far, the highest wind speed ever recorded there was 199 mph (320 km/h).

CHAPTER 3

NATURAL RESOURCES

Scientists think Antarctica could hold valuable **minerals**. It is possible the continent has silver, copper, gold, coal, and more. But no country has tried to dig them out. Antarctica is too cold, and the thick ice makes it too difficult.

Whales and seals were once hunted in the waters off Antarctica. Whales were used for their meat and oils. Seals were used for their fur. These animals were almost wiped out. Today parts of the ocean are protected zones. No hunting is allowed there.

CHAPTER 4
PLANTS AND ANIMALS

No polar bears live in Antarctica—they are Arctic animals.

PLANTS

Plants that live in Antarctica must survive freezing temperatures. They must grow with little sunlight or water. That is why no trees or bushes grow in Antarctica.

Some mosses and lichens live on the continent's rocks. They are able to go **dormant** in winter. Then they grow quickly during the short summer. They survive on water from melting snow and ice.

PENGUINS

Penguins live in Antarctica and on surrounding islands. Their feathers and layers of fat keep them warm. Penguins can't fly, but they swim well. They dive below the ice to catch fish. Penguins dive deeper than any other bird on Earth.

Emperor penguins huddle in groups to stay warm. They are the only penguin that hatch chicks during the winter. The parent covers the chick to keep it from freezing.

SEALS

Seals have a layer of **blubber** that keeps them warm. Some **species** also have fur. Seals hunt for fish under the sea ice. They leave the water and spend time on the land or ice to raise their pups.

ANIMALS IN THE OCEAN

The continent's seas are full of life. Antarctic krill are about the size of a jumbo paper clip. These small animals eat microscopic plants. Many bigger sea creatures eat krill. Whales, seals, fish, and penguins feed on them.

Krill swim together in huge numbers. Some krill swarms are so large they have been seen from space.

Some fish do well in cold ocean waters. Antarctic cod and toothfish have a kind of antifreeze in their blood that keeps them from freezing.

Ten species of whales live in Antarctica's waters. They **migrate** to warmer seas in the winter. Orca hunt fish, penguins, and seals. Humpback whales have a hairy plate in their mouths. They use it to catch krill and other tiny sea creatures.

CHAPTER 5

EXPLORING ANTARCTICA

Ancient peoples suspected a continent sat at the bottom of the world. Some **Indigenous** peoples of Polynesia told stories about explorers seeing a frozen land. In the 1800s, European and American explorers searched for it. Their countries wanted to be the first to claim it.

Russian Fabian Gottlieb von Bellingshausen was one of the first Europeans to explore Antarctica.

Explorers also went to Antarctica for science. But early Antarctic exploration was difficult and dangerous. Ice trapped and crushed ships. Stranded explorers had no shelter, food, or water. Many died.

RACE TO THE SOUTH POLE

In 1911, two explorers wanted to be the first to reach the South Pole. Robert Scott was a British explorer and had tried to reach it once before. Roald Amundsen was a Norwegian explorer who thought his team could be the first. Amundsen's team beat Scott's to the South Pole by 33 days. Amundsen made it back. Unfortunately, Scott and his team died in Antarctica.

None of the British Antarctic Expedition of 1911 survived.

The invention of airplanes opened up more of Antarctica. In 1947, the United States sent an expedition with more than 4,700 people, 13 ships, and two planes. They photographed most of the coast to make maps. By 1958, 12 nations had set up more than 60 research stations on Antarctica.

CHAPTER 6
ANTARCTICA TODAY

No one nation owns Antarctica. In 1959, 12 countries signed the Antarctic Treaty. The countries agreed that the continent should only be used for peaceful purposes. They also agreed that any country may do scientific research there. Research must be shared with everyone. Today, 54 countries have signed the treaty.

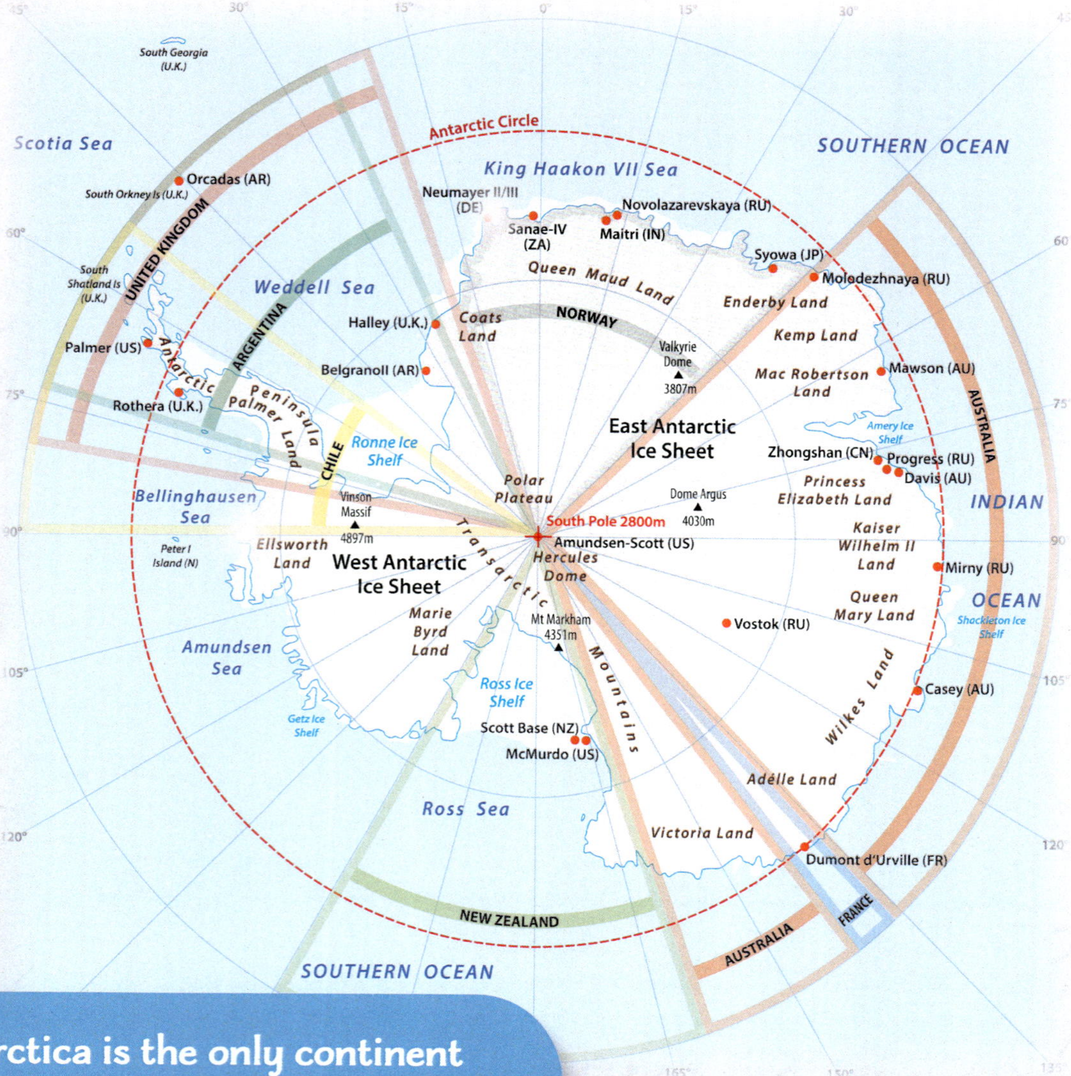

Antarctica is the only continent without any countries.

Few people stay all winter. Most scientists and visitors come in the summer months, from October to March.

No Indigenous peoples ever lived on Antarctica. No settlers ever built towns and cities. But there are research stations on the continent. Scientists come and work there for months at a time. Tourists also visit Antarctica.

McMURDO STATION

McMurdo Station is owned by the United States. It is the largest station on the continent. McMurdo is nearly a town. It has more than 100 buildings and a post office. The people who work there are scientists, or they help run the station. None live there permanently.

The coldest recorded temperature at McMurdo Station was -59°F (-50°C).

CONCORDIA STATION

Concordia Station is owned by France and Italy. It is the most remote station on Earth. No sun shines for four months out of the year. The average temperature is -94°F (-70°C). It can house a crew of up to 16. Scientists may stay there for about a year as they study the continent.

Antarctica is a frozen continent like nowhere else on Earth!

GLOSSARY

blubber (BLUH-br): The thick layer of fat on whales, seals, and some other sea animals

climate (KLAI-muht): The usual weather conditions in a certain region or area

dormant (DOR-muhnt): A period when a living thing does not grow or move to save energy

equator (EE-kway-tr): An imaginary line around the middle of Earth that is the same distance from the North Pole to the South Pole

Indigenous (in-DIH-juh-nuhs): The first people who lived in a region

interior (in-TEE-ree-ur): The part of a country or region that is far from the coast

migrate (MY-grayt): To move from one place to another when the season changes

mineral (MIH-nuh-rl): A solid substance that is formed naturally under the ground

peninsula (puh-NIN-suh-luh): A piece of land almost completely surrounded by water but that is attached to a larger land area

species (SPEE-sheez or SPEE-sees): A group of animals or plants that are alike in certain ways

INDEX

Antarctic Treaty 26

explorer 22–24

iceberg 4, 11

krill 20–21

Lake Vostok 8

McMurdo Station 28

mountain 8–9

penguin 4, 13, 18, 20–21

seal 15, 19–21

whale 15, 20–21

COMPREHENSION QUESTIONS

1. How many people live in Antarctica permanently?

a. 200

b. 1,000

c. None

2. Which animal lives in Antarctica?

a. Polar bear

b. Penguin

c. Wolf

3. Which Antarctic research station is the largest?

a. Vinson Station

b. Concordia Station

c. McMurdo Station

4. True or False: The equator runs through Antarctica.

5. True of False: Antarctica is the only continent without any countries.

Answers: 1. C, 2. B, 3. C, 4. False, 5. True

ABOUT THE AUTHOR

Tracy Vonder Brink loves true stories and facts. She has written more than 20 books for kids and is a contributing editor for three children's science magazines. Tracy lives in Cincinnati, Ohio, with her husband, two daughters, and two rescue dogs.

Crabtree Publishing

crabtreebooks.com 800-387-7650

Written by: Tracy Vonder Brink
Cover design by: Kathy Walsh
Interior design by: Kathy Walsh
Series Development: James Earley
Proofreader: Crystal Sikkens
Educational Consultant: Marie Lemke M.Ed.
Production manager: Candice Campbell
Prepress technician: Katherine Kantor

Hardcover	978-1-0396-6051-9
Paperback	978-1-0396-6246-9
Ebook (pdf)	978-1-0396-7042-6
Epub	978-1-0396-7240-6
Read-along	978-1-0396-7438-7
Audio book	978-1-0396-7636-7

Printed in the U.S.A./CP072026

Published in Canada
Crabtree Publishing
616 Welland Avenue
St. Catharines, Ontario
L2M 5V6

Published in the United States
Crabtree Publishing
347 Fifth Avenue
Suite 1402-145
New York, NY 10016

Photographs: Shutterstock; Cover: ©Triff, ©Khurasan, ©nypl, @Dima_designer, ©slowmotiongli; Title Pg: ©Triff, ©Dima_designer; Pg 3-31: ©Triff; Pg 4-31: ©Neti.OneLove; Pg 4: ©Ethan Daniels; Pg 6: ©66 north on Unsplash; Pg 7: ©robert mcgillivray, ©Victor Maschek; Pg 8: ©Konstantin Grosch 1986; Pg 9: ©Danita Delimont; Pg 10: ©Matt Makes Photos; Pg 11: ©Evgeny Kovalev spb; Pg 12: ©Earth Trotter Photography; Pg 13: ©Ondrej Prosicky; Pg 14: ©Alexey Suloev; Pg 15: ©Philipp Salveter; Pg 16: ©Emily Gamertsfelder; Pg 17: ©Pataporn Kuanui; Pg 18: ©vladsilver, ©Roger ARPS BPE1 CPAGB; Pg 19: ©Volodymyr Goinyk; Pg 20: ©Andrea Izzotti, @Wiki; Pg 21: ©vladsilver; Pg 22: @Wiki; Pg 23: ©Library of Congress; Pg 24: @Wiki; Pg 25: ©Library of Congress; Pg 26: ©Rainer Lesniewski; Pg 27: ©axily; Pg 28: ©Eli Duke flckr; Pg 29: ©NSA

Library and Archives Canada Cataloguing in Publication
Available at the Library and Archives Canada

Library of Congress Cataloging-in-Publication Data
Available at the Library of Congress